Managing Virtual Infrastructure with Veeam® ONE™

Discover ways to manage your virtual infrastructure with Veeam® ONE™ in a development environment

Kevin L. Sapp

[PACKT] enterprise
PUBLISHING
professional expertise distilled

BIRMINGHAM - MUMBAI

Managing Virtual Infrastructure with Veeam® ONE™

First published: December 2014

Production reference: 1191214

Published by Packt Publishing Ltd.
Livery Place
35 Livery Street
Birmingham B3 2PB, UK.

ISBN 978-1-78217-379-3

www.packtpub.com

Credits

Author
Kevin L. Sapp

Reviewers
Davide Benvegnù
James Bowling
Steve Dolphin

Commissioning Editor
Ashwin Nair

Acquisition Editor
Neha Nagwekar

Content Development Editor
Akashdeep Kundu

Technical Editors
Novina Kewalramani
Edwin Moses

Copy Editors
Roshni Banerjee
Pranjali Chury

Project Coordinator
Neha Thakur

Proofreaders
Simran Bhogal
Maria Gould
Ameesha Green
Paul Hindle

Indexers
Mariammal Chettiyar
Monica Ajmera Mehta

Production Coordinator
Nilesh R. Mohite

Cover Work
Nilesh R. Mohite

About the Author

Kevin L. Sapp has worked in the IT industry for over 5 years. After graduating from Florida State University with a Bachelor of Science degree in Management Information Systems, he started working for a Fortune 100 company as a systems engineer. This helped him gain technical experience in supporting and managing over 15,000 systems in retail and corporate environments. He is the author of the book *Instant VMWare Player for Virtualization, Packt Publishing*, and the CEO of the company CodeDuet, LLC, which develops mobile applications.

I would like to thank my family and friends who have supported me over the years: the Sapp family (Ashely, Allison, and Adonis), my fiancée Janay, and my friend Emerson Auguste from Lakeland. Without their help, I would not be doing what I do today, and it is because of them and others whom I may not have listed here that I feel compelled to pass my knowledge on to those willing to learn.

About the Reviewers

Davide Benvegnù is the International Development Manager for Aruba, the biggest Italian web services provider. With over 10 years of experience in software development and IT, he is currently responsible for the management of software development. He works with Azure and does Application Lifecycle Management (ALM). In the past, in addition to software development, he has also managed and coordinated the systems administration and dealt with virtualization and consolidation of entire data centers.

Davide has also been a freelancer since 2009 under the brand DBTek, and he makes web and desktop applications and Windows Store and Windows Phone apps as well as acts as a consultant in the field of ALM.

He is a member of the staff of DotNetToscana, an official Microsoft Technical Community, where he helps to organize events and gives speeches at technical conferences about .NET and the Microsoft technology stack. He has conducted several sessions and talks at events of national relevance, such as Community Days, SMAU, Festival ICT, and many others.

He has several IT-related certifications (issued by VMware, Veeam®, Microsoft, and others). He always keeps himself up to date with the advances in the field of technology and tries to transfer his knowledge and passion through the talks and courses he participates in as a trainer.

James Bowling is a VCAP5-DCD, VCAP5-DCA, VCP-Cloud, EMCCIS/EMCCA, VMware vExpert (x4), Cisco Champion for Data Center, PernixPro, Houston VMUG Leader, and virtualization enthusiast living in Houston, Texas. He has over 15 years of experience. He received the 2009 COMMON/IBM Power Systems Innovation Award for Energy Efficiency for his design and implementation of the United States Bowling Congress (USBC) Datacenter in Arlington, Texas. He has given presentations at VMworld US and EMEA about automation and orchestration. His experience spans designing, deploying, and maintaining large-scale cloud infrastructures. He is currently the Principal Consultant for Data Center Practice at General Datatech in Dallas, Texas. He can be reached on Twitter (@vSential) or through his virtualization blog at http://vsential.com/.

Steve Dolphin is an experienced solutions architect who's been working in the professional services sector for over 10 years. His extensive experience with a range of hardware and software platforms ideally locates him for a wide range of business projects and consultancy. He can be contacted via his website, www.stephendolphin.co.uk.

www.PacktPub.com

Support files, eBooks, discount offers, and more

For support files and downloads related to your book, please visit www.PacktPub.com.

Did you know that Packt offers eBook versions of every book published, with PDF and ePub files available? You can upgrade to the eBook version at www.PacktPub.com and as a print book customer, you are entitled to a discount on the eBook copy. Get in touch with us at service@packtpub.com for more details.

At www.PacktPub.com, you can also read a collection of free technical articles, sign up for a range of free newsletters and receive exclusive discounts and offers on Packt books and eBooks.

https://www.packtpub.com/books/subscription/packtlib

Do you need instant solutions to your IT questions? PacktLib is Packt's online digital book library. Here, you can search, access, and read Packt's entire library of books.

Why subscribe?

- Fully searchable across every book published by Packt
- Copy and paste, print, and bookmark content
- On demand and accessible via a web browser

Free access for Packt account holders

If you have an account with Packt at www.PacktPub.com, you can use this to access PacktLib today and view 9 entirely free books. Simply use your login credentials for immediate access.

Instant updates on new Packt books

Get notified! Find out when new books are published by following @PacktEnterprise on Twitter or the *Packt Enterprise* Facebook page.

Table of Contents

Preface

Welcome to *Managing Virtual Infrastructure with Veeam® ONE™*. Have you always wondered about ways to monitor, manage, and analyze virtual environments? Well, you are in the right place. This book serves as an easy guide to learn about a virtual machine monitoring tool called Veeam® ONE™. This tool offers an assortment of benefits to large enterprise environments by collecting data from hypervisors and making that information visible to system administrators in real time. The concepts discussed in this book will give you the skills needed to confidently deploy the Veeam® ONE™ application to your virtualized environment.

What this book covers

Chapter 1, Getting Started with Veeam® ONE™, explains the process used to download and access the prerequisites needed to begin using the Veeam® ONE™ application.

Chapter 2, Configuring Veeam® ONE™ Monitoring, covers the process used to configure the Veeam® ONE™ Monitor.

Chapter 3, Configuring Veeam® ONE™ Reports, covers the process of saving, viewing, and configuring the Veeam® ONE™ reports.

Chapter 4, Veeam® ONE™ Business View, explains how to use the business view to plan, control, and analyze changes in the virtual environment.

Chapter 5, Best Practices, covers some of the steps used to troubleshoot the common issues on host and guest systems.

What you need for this book

You will need a server that meets the minimum requirements outlined here:

- CPU: modern x64 processor (minimum two cores)
- RAM: 4096 MB (minimum) and 8198 MB (recommended)

Also, access to the Internet will be required to download the Veeam® ONE™ application and license key.

Who this book is for

This book is intended for business users and virtualization administrators who want to know how to monitor their virtual environment using Veeam® ONE™. In this book, you will find the steps to install Veeam® ONE™, view and create dashboards, and troubleshoot your virtual environment with minimal effort.

Conventions

In this book, you will find a number of styles of text that distinguish between different kinds of information. Here are some examples of these styles and an explanation of their meaning.

Code words in text, database table names, folder names, filenames, file extensions, pathnames, dummy URLs, user input, and Twitter handles are shown as follows: "Save the `VeeamONE.iso` file."

New terms and **important words** are shown in bold. Words that you see on the screen, in menus or dialog boxes for example, appear in the text like this: "Click on the **Veeam ONE for VMware and Hyper-V** link."

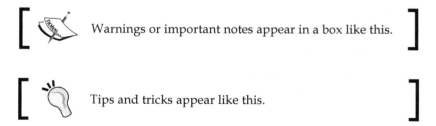

[Warnings or important notes appear in a box like this.]

[Tips and tricks appear like this.]

Reader feedback

Feedback from our readers is always welcome. Let us know what you think about this book—what you liked or may have disliked. Reader feedback is important for us to develop titles that you really get the most out of.

To send us general feedback, simply send an e-mail to feedback@packtpub.com, and mention the book title via the subject of your message.

If there is a topic that you have expertise in and you are interested in either writing or contributing to a book, see our author guide on www.packtpub.com/authors.

Customer support

Now that you are the proud owner of a Packt book, we have a number of things to help you to get the most from your purchase.

Downloading the example code

You can download the example code files for all Packt books you have purchased from your account at http://www.packtpub.com. If you purchased this book elsewhere, you can visit http://www.packtpub.com/support and register to have the files e-mailed directly to you.

Errata

Although we have taken every care to ensure the accuracy of our content, mistakes do happen. If you find a mistake in one of our books—maybe a mistake in the text or the code—we would be grateful if you would report this to us. By doing so, you can save other readers from frustration and help us improve subsequent versions of this book. If you find any errata, please report them by visiting http://www.packtpub.com/submit-errata, selecting your book, clicking on the **errata submission form** link, and entering the details of your errata. Once your errata are verified, your submission will be accepted and the errata will be uploaded on our website, or added to any list of existing errata, under the Errata section of that title. Any existing errata can be viewed by selecting your title from http://www.packtpub.com/support.

Piracy

Piracy of copyright material on the Internet is an ongoing problem across all media. At Packt, we take the protection of our copyright and licenses very seriously. If you come across any illegal copies of our works, in any form, on the Internet, please provide us with the location address or website name immediately so that we can pursue a remedy.

Please contact us at copyright@packtpub.com with a link to the suspected pirated material.

We appreciate your help in protecting our authors, and our ability to bring you valuable content.

Questions

You can contact us at questions@packtpub.com if you are having a problem with any aspect of the book, and we will do our best to address it.

1

Getting Started with Veeam® ONE™

Veeam® ONE™ is an application that is used to support and monitor virtual machines in a virtualized environment. It allows system administrators to create, configure, and display reporting mechanisms used to survey machines housed by Hyper-V or VMware ESX hypervisors in a laboratory or enterprise infrastructure. In order for Veeam® ONE™ to operate properly, there are several operating system, network, and hardware requirements that must be met. This chapter will explain the process used to download and access the prerequisites needed to begin using Veeam® ONE™.

In this chapter, we will cover the following topics:

- Downloading Veeam® ONE™
- The prerequisites for Veeam® ONE™
- Veeam® ONE™ free versus full edition
- Installing Veeam® ONE™

Downloading Veeam® ONE™

The following steps explain the process of downloading and installing the Veeam® ONE™ application. You need to create a Veeam® account and download the source files needed to install the Veeam® ONE™ application.

1. Register for a Veeam® ONE™ account.
2. Navigate to `http://www.veeam.com/downloads/`.

3. Click on the **Veeam ONE for VMware and Hyper-V** link.

4. Click on **Download**. Go to the download page and click on the **Download** button.

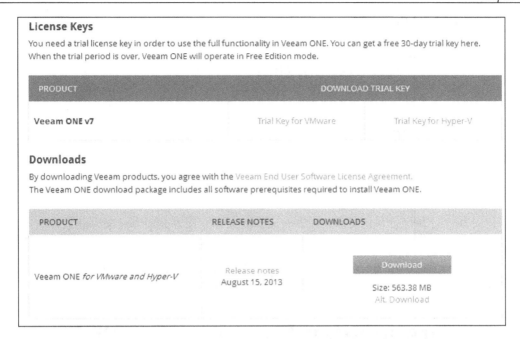

5. Read the Veeam End User Software License Agreement document and click on **Accept**.

6. Save the `VeeamONE.iso` file.

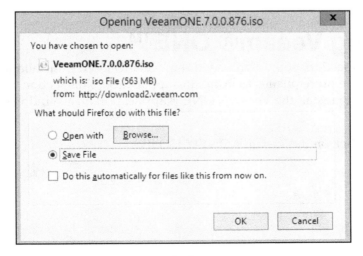

7. Download the trial license key.

 License Sent

License for Veeam ONE for Hyper-V was sent to your email.
It should arrive in few minutes.

If you do not receive it please:
- Check your junk or spam mail folder.
- Contact Veeam Support support@veeam.com.

Close

Now that you have the license key available, the next section will explain the process of installing Veeam® ONE™ on a Windows server.

The prerequisites for Veeam® ONE™

The following section will explain the Veeam® ONE™ hardware and software requirements. Please use the link as a reference guide for items such as hard disk space or memory that must meet the minimum requirements outlined by Veeam® ONE™.

For more information on Veeam® ONE™ prerequisites, visit `http://veeampdf.s3.amazonaws.com/release_notes/veeam_one_7_release_notes.pdf?AWSAccessKeyId=AKIAJI4MX44AEVG3NBLA&Expires=1413842990&Signature=hkQe51TTbtw8y2QeVFc9okufz0o%3D`.

Installing Veeam® ONE™

In the previous section, you downloaded the Veeam® ONE™ installation ISO file and reviewed the prerequisites to install the application. This section will explain the procedures to install the Veeam® ONE™ application on a Windows 2012 Server as follows:

1. Right-click on the Veeam® ONE™ ISO file.

2. Select the **Mount** option.

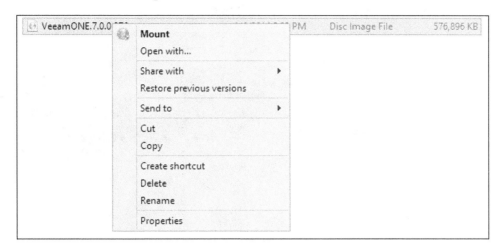

 If you are using the Windows Server operating system 2008 R2, you will need to extract the ISO file using the WinRAR or 7-Zip archive manager utility applications.

3. Now that the ISO file has been mounted, the following folder structure will be shown. Click on **Setup**.

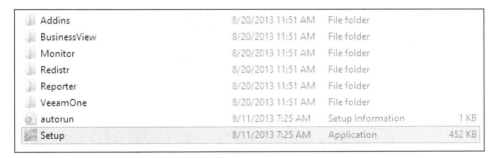

 The folder structure shown in the preceding screenshot is subject to change due to adjustments made to the ISO file by Veeam® through software revisions.

4. The Veeam® ONE™ installation window is shown in the following screenshot. Click on **Veeam® ONE™ Server**.

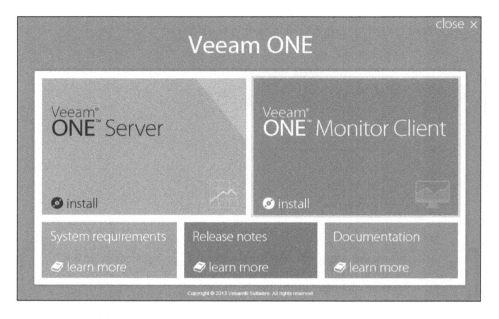

5. You will be prompted to install Microsoft Visual C++ 2010 Service Pack 1 Redistributable Package. Click on **OK**.

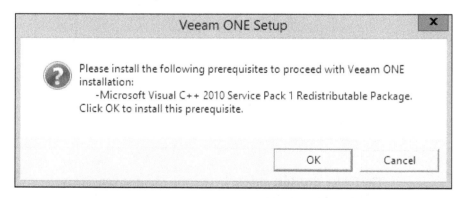

6. The **Veeam ONE Setup** page will be shown. Click on **Next**.

7. Accept the license agreement and click on **Next**.

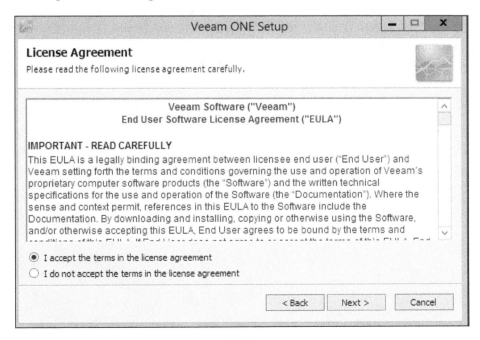

8. Go to the Veeam® ONE™ website and download the Veeam® ONE™ license file.

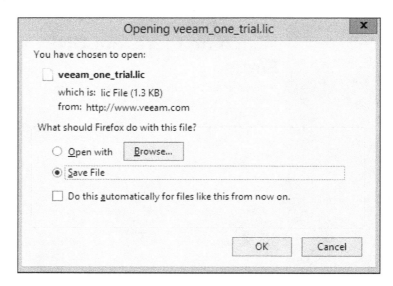

9. Navigate to **Provide License | Full functionality mode**, click on **Browse…**, and select the Veeam® ONE™ license key that has been sent by e-mail or can be downloaded.

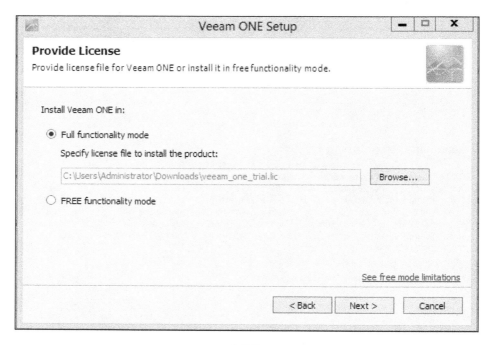

10. Click on **Next**.

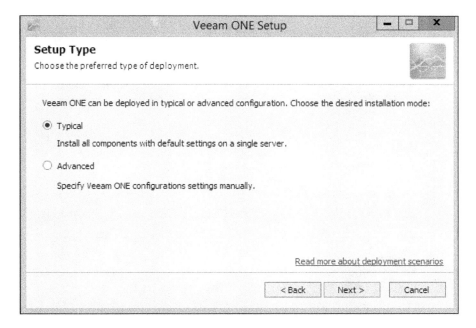

11. The prerequisites check will start. Then, click on **Install** to deploy the missing features.

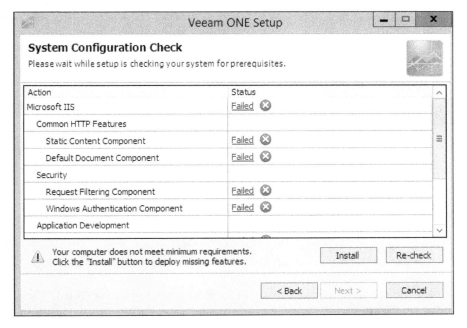

12. The **System Configuration Check** dialog box will change the status to **Passed**. Click on **Next** to continue.

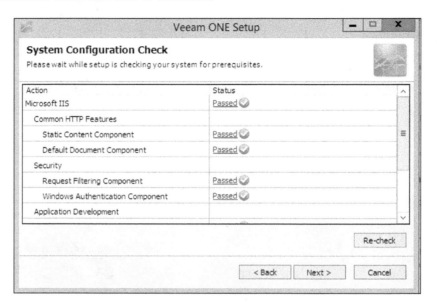

13. Check the default installation path and click on **Next**.

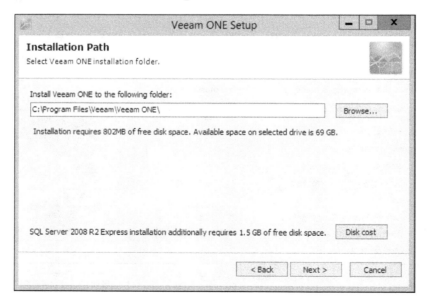

14. Enter the credentials of a local administrator or domain account. Then, click on **Next**.

 For security reasons, it is suggested that you use a domain account for this installation instead of the local administrator credentials.

15. Click on **Next** to install a new local SQL instance.

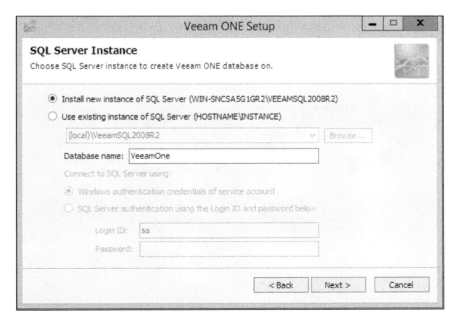

16. Check the default port settings and click on **Next**.

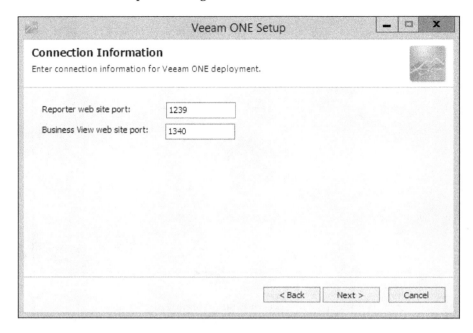

17. Click on **Skip virtual infrastructure configuration**. We will discuss this subject matter in the upcoming chapters.

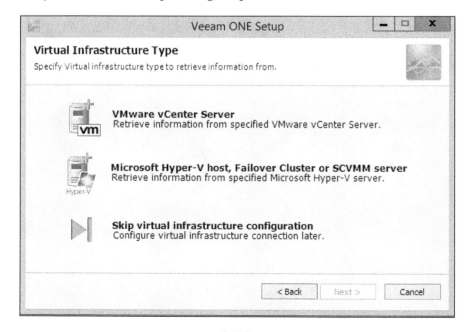

18. Click on **Install** to begin the Veeam® ONE™ installation.

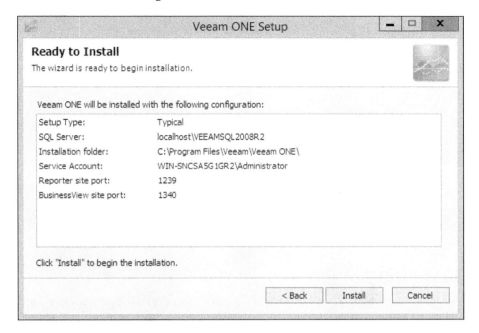

19. Click on **Finish**.

20. Click on **Yes** to log off and complete the installation.

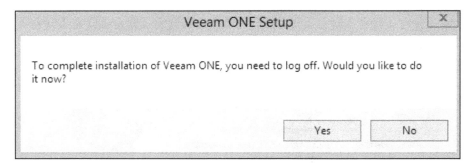

You have just completed the installation process for Veeam® ONE™. The following section will provide further details on the features and components of Veeam® ONE™.

Downloads

The free edition of Veeam® ONE™ includes all of the core components of the Veeam® ONE™ application, which includes data collection, multiuser support, dashboards, and a Microsoft SQL Server backend. When you purchase a Full Edition license, the following components are unlocked:

- Monitoring and management for guest processes
- All predefined reporting dashboards
- Automation for report production and distribution

- Extended monitoring, reporting, and capacity planning for Veeam® Backup and Replication, as shown in the following screenshot:

Feature	Description	Free Edition restrictions
General		
Deployment scenarios	Install all Veeam ONE components on the same physical or virtual server, or choose the advanced deployment option for a distributed installation.	Advanced deployment option is not available.
Performance data	View and analyze historical performance data to understand trends and facilitate troubleshooting of performance issues.	The monitoring console displays data for the last 7 days, and performance reports are limited to data for the previous 24 hours.
Integration with Backup & Replication		
Advanced monitoring, reporting and capacity planning	Leverage advanced capabilities in Veeam ONE to monitor the performance and status of your backup jobs, report on protected and unprotected VMs, discover and monitor backup readiness and repository requirements, and more.	Capabilities limited to infrastructure assessment tools for estimating VM change rates and validating configuration settings.
Monitoring and alarms		
Email notification for alarms	Receive notification of alarms via customizable email.	Email customization options are not available, and the email does not include all alarm details, such as time and affected object.
Custom alarms	Ensure complete monitoring coverage by creating custom alarms for events that are unique to your virtual environment.	Not available
Alarm modeling	Model an alarm against past performance data to understand potential alarm frequency and avoid issues like inadvertent alert storms and missed events.	Not available

Let's get acquainted with some useful resources. To do so, you can:

- Refer to the following link for the Veeam® ONE™ release notes:

  `http://www.veeam.com/veeam_one_7_whats_new_en_wn.pdf`

- Refer to the following link for the Veeam® ONE™ downloads:

  `http://www.veeam.com/downloads/`

- Refer to the following link to download Microsoft Visual C++ 2010 Service Pack 1 Redistributable Package from the Microsoft website:

  `http://www.microsoft.com/en-us/download/details.aspx?id=14632`

Summary

This chapter explained the process of downloading and accessing the documentation needed to start using Veeam® ONE™. You were able to download Veeam® ONE™ and install it on a Windows machine using the system prerequisites provided by Veeam®.

In the next chapter, we will discuss how to get started with the Veeam® ONE™ application and some of its exciting features.

2
Configuring Veeam® ONE™ Monitoring

Veeam® ONE™ provides a robust monitoring solution to view real-time alerts for the backend and performance issues. The benefit of having this tool is that it reduces the number of steps for data collection from multiple IT entities, such as networking and database administration staff, so that top-level IT professionals can have maximum visibility of their virtual environment. It takes the guesswork out of troubleshooting performance and availability issues in a virtual infrastructure. This chapter will explain the process used to configure Veeam® ONE™ Monitor.

In this chapter, we will cover the following topics:

- The Veeam® ONE™ Monitor interface
- Monitoring tasks and events
- Viewing the dashboards when monitoring
- Configuring the notifications

The Veeam® ONE™ Monitor interface

The Veeam® ONE™ Monitor interface has several options and configurations that should be set up in order to add value to the application.

The following screenshot shows the toolbar menu:

The navigation buttons

The following navigation buttons are available on the Veeam® ONE™ Monitor console. A description of each button component is as follows:

- **Back**: This button navigates to the previous view of the Veeam® ONE™ Monitor console.

- **Forward**: This button navigates to the next view of the Veeam® ONE™ Monitor console.

- **Refresh**: This button updates the information shown in the Veeam® ONE™ Monitor console. Press *F5* for the keyboard shortcut.

- **Add Server**: This button creates a connection to a new host server. Press *CTRL + I* for the keyboard shortcut.

- **Notifications**: This button configures the notification settings using **Configuration Wizard**.

- **Reports**: This button creates a report for a selected object in the inventory pane.

- **Modelling**: This button configures the number of alerts that will occur for a virtual infrastructure object.

- **Options**: This button changes the Veeam® ONE™ client or server settings.

- **Help**: This button is used to view the Veeam® ONE™ help logfiles and license information. Press *F1* for the keyboard shortcut.

- **Full Screen**: This button enables the fullscreen mode for the Veeam® ONE™ console. Press *F11* for the keyboard shortcut.

- **Search**: This button is used to look for a business view, virtual infrastructure, or backup component.

The inventory pane

The inventory pane shows a hierarchy of objects for the virtual infrastructure components. The content of the information displayed changes based on the object that you select from the inventory pane.

You can hide and reveal the inventory pane by clicking on the collapse/expand box on the left-hand side of each hierarchy node.

In order to view the errors and warning in the hierarchy, right-click on the node in the inventory pane and select **Show all error objects** from the shortcut menu.

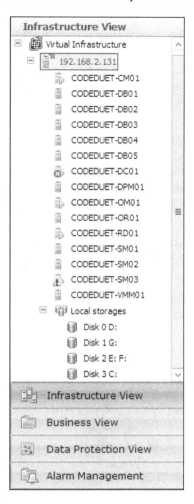

The inventory pane is located on the left-hand side of the Veeam® ONE™ Monitor console. Each node in the hierarchy shows the state and alarm of the infrastructure objects. The inventory pane includes the following items:

- **Infrastructure View**
- **Business View**
- **Data Protection View**
- **Alarm Management**

Infrastructure View

The **Infrastructure View** item of the inventory pane shows the host IP address/name and each of the monitored servers, clusters, virtual machines, storages, and other monitored objects (shown in the preceding screenshot).

 This is a depiction of the Hyper-V environment. In the VMware environment, the storages are called **Datastores** in this view.

Business View

The **Business View** item of the inventory pane shows a categorized list of the reports for virtual machines, host systems, data stores, and clusters. The infrastructure topology is intended to make it easier to find monitored objects based on their business function.

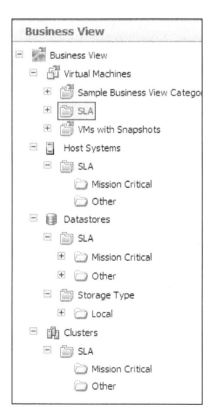

The **Business View** item is a great tool to organize monitors and reports into categories. For example, all of the exchange servers on your environment can be added to a mission-critical SLA for easy monitoring and reporting.

Data Protection View

The **Data Protection View** item of the inventory pane shows a list of the connected Veeam® **Backup & Replication** servers, which allows you to see the status and performance of the data protection components.

Alarm Management

The **Alarm Management** view of the inventory pane shows a list of the predefined alarms for each infrastructure technology, **VMware** and **Hyper-V**. From this pane, you can manage the alarms and their trigger conditions and enable and disable the alarms.

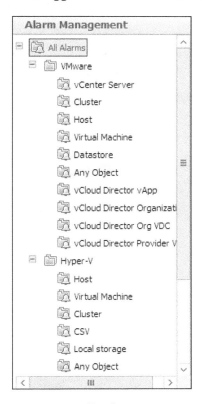

Monitoring tasks and events

The **Tasks & Events** dashboard displays the different levels of events that have occurred in your virtual environment. To view the list of tasks and events, select the inventory panel and click on the **Tasks & Events** tab. By default, the **Tasks & Events** view only displays data per hour. To change this, select the desired interval from the **Events from** listbox. To look for a particular event, enter the event description in the **Search** field.

The following details are available under the **Tasks & Events** dashboard:

- Event type (**User, Info, Warning,** or **Error**)
- Event target
- Time of occurrence
- A short event description
- Object that caused or initiated the event

As you click on each event in the list, the event description will be displayed in the **Event Details** section at the bottom of the dashboard.

Use the **Export...** button that is located next to the search field to save the events to a CSV file.

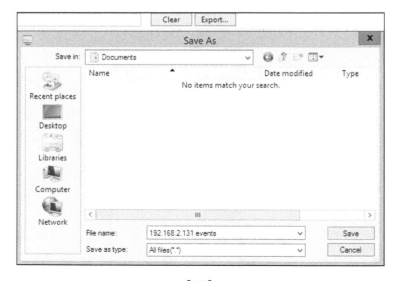

This section discussed the monitoring tasks and events as well as the steps to export information. Next, we will discuss the CPU performance charts.

Viewing the CPU performance charts

The CPU performance charts are used to show the processor utilization on the machines in your virtual environment. This is useful to view the amount of CPU resources consumed during the backup jobs or other resource intensive tasks.

Select the **Display known events** checkbox at the bottom of the performance chart. Then, click on the **Advanced** link beside the **Display known events** checkbox. You will be able to view the events for VM live migration, snapshot creation and removal, and Veeam® backup and replication.

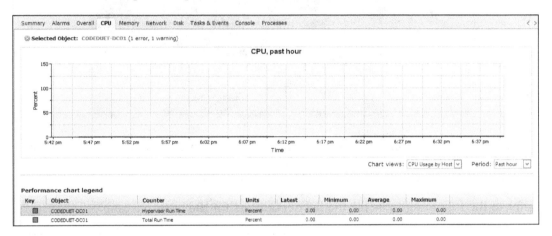

To view the virtual machine from the console, perform the following steps:

1. Select the inventory panel and click on the **Console** tab.
2. If prompted, enter the local administrator credentials or login credentials used to access the Hyper-V server.

The login was successful!

After you log in, you will be able to view the virtual machine from the Veeam® ONE™ console. This will allow you to streamline the process of resolving the server issues.

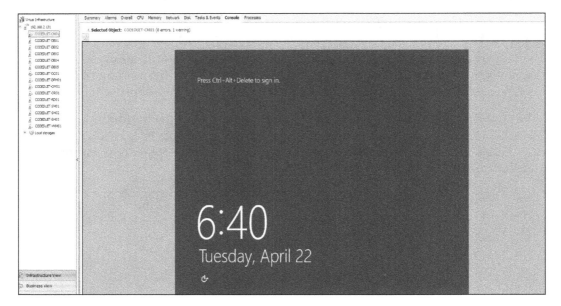

In order to view the memory performance chart, click on the **Memory** tab to display the virtual memory statistics for each object. The performance chart legend shows the information on the counters used for each view.

Refer to the following table for the list of counters for the host machine:

Chart views	Counter(s)	Description
Memory Usage	**Hyper-V Services Memory Consumed**	This counter shows the bytes of memory currently used by the host services
	Hyper-V Services Memory Usage	This counter shows the percentage of memory currently used by the host services
	Memory Consumed	This counter shows the bytes of memory used on the host machine
	Memory Usage	This counter shows the percentage of memory used by the host

Chart views	Counter(s)	Description
Memory Swap Faults	Page Faults/sec	This counter shows the page faults as each process attempts to read from virtual memory that is marked as **unavailable**
	Page Reads/sec	This counter shows the rate that memory is written to the pagefile on the hard disk due to memory shortage
Committed Memory	Committed Bytes	This counter shows the amount of bytes allocated by each process and committed to the RAM or pagefile
Memory Pressure	Average Pressure	This counter shows the percentage of memory available on the host machine
Memory Swap Rate	Page Writes/sec	This counter shows the number of times the data was written to a pagefile
	Pages Input/sec	This counter shows the rate of pagefile reads
	Pages Output/sec	This counter shows the rate of pagefile writes
	Pages/sec	This counter shows the frequency of pagefile storage and retrieval

- The **Memory Usage** counter(s):
    - **Hyper-V Services Memory Consumed**: This counter shows the bytes of memory currently used by the host services
    - **Hyper-V Services Memory Usage**: This counter shows the percentage of memory currently used by the host services
    - **Memory Consumed**: This counter shows the bytes of memory used on the host machine
    - **Memory Usage**: This counter shows the percentage of memory used by the host

- The **Memory Swap Faults** counter(s):
    - **Page Faults/sec**: This counter shows the page faults as each process attempts to read from virtual memory that is marked as **unavailable**.
    - **Page Reads/sec**: This counter shows how often memory is written to the pagefile on the hard disk due to memory shortage

- The **Committed Memory** counter(s):

  ° **Committed Bytes**: This counter shows the amount of bytes allocated by each process and committed to the RAM or pagefile.

- The **Memory Pressure** counter(s):

  ° **Average Pressure**:- This counter shows the percentage of memory available on the host machine

- The **Memory Swap Rate** counter(s):

  ° **Page Writes/sec**: This counter shows the number of times the data was written to a pagefile

  ° **Pages Input/sec**: This counter shows the rate of pagefile reads

  ° **Pages Output/sec**: This counter shows the rate of pagefile writes

  ° **Pages/sec**: This counter shows the frequency of pagefile storage and retrieval

Refer to the following table for the list of counters for the virtual machine:

Chart views	Counter(s)	Description
Memory Usage	Guest Visible Physical Memory	This counter shows the amount of memory allocated to a virtual machine
	Physical Memory	This counter shows the amount of memory in the virtual machine
Memory Pressure	Demand	This counter shows the amount of memory needed by the virtual machines for all active processes
	Current Pressure	This counter shows the percentage of memory that a virtual machine needs versus what is available

- The **Memory Usage** counter(s):

  ° **Guest Visible Physical Memory**: This counter shows the amount of memory allocated to a virtual machine

  ° **Physical Memory**: This counter shows the amount of memory available in the virtual machine

- The **Memory Pressure** counter(s):

  ° **Demand**: This counter shows the amount of memory needed by the virtual machines for all active processes

○ **Current Pressure:** This counter shows the percentage of memory that a virtual machine needs versus what is available

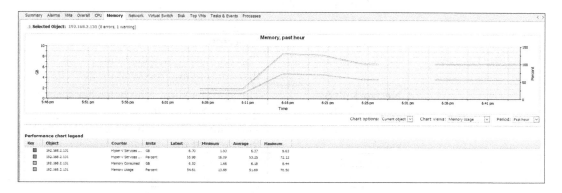

The Network performance chart

The **Network** chart comes with the predefined chart views. This information is useful when you need to figure out which virtual machines are consuming excessive network bandwidth and when troubleshooting performance problems.

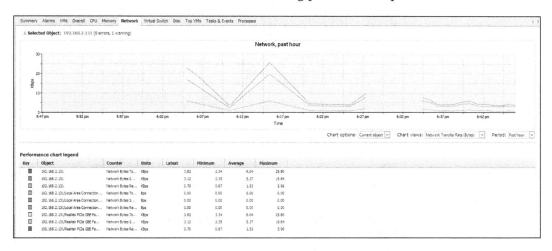

The network performance chart comes with the predefined information, as shown in the preceding screenshot. This allows an IT administrator to troubleshoot and analyze the network issues shown by looking at the historical data.

Chart features	Counters	Description
Network Transfer Rate	**Network Bytes Total**	This counter shows the bytes per second that are sent and received on the NIC
	Network Bytes Received/sec	This counter shows the bytes per second that are received on the NIC
	Network Bytes Sent/ sec	This counter shows the bytes per second that are sent from the NIC
Network Output Queue Length	**Network Bytes Total**	This counter shows the bytes per second that are sent and received on the NIC
	Network Bytes Received/sec	This counter shows the bytes per second that are received on the NIC
	Network Bytes Sent/ sec	This counter shows the bytes per second that are sent from the NIC
Network Connections	**Network Bytes Total**	This counter shows the bytes per second that are sent and received on the NIC
	Network Bytes Received/sec	This counter shows the bytes per second that are received on the NIC
	Network Bytes Sent/ sec	This counter shows the bytes per second that are sent from the NIC
Network Errors	**Network Bytes Total**	This counter shows the bytes per second that are sent and received on the NIC
	Network Bytes Received/sec	This counter shows the bytes per second that are received on the NIC
	Network Bytes Sent/ sec	This counter shows the bytes per second that are sent from the NIC
Network Transfer Rate (Packets)	**Network Bytes Total**	This counter shows the bytes per second that are sent and received on the NIC
	Network Bytes Received/sec	This counter shows the bytes per second that are received on the NIC
	Network Bytes Sent/ sec	This counter shows the bytes per second that are sent from the NIC
Network Transfer Rate (Packets)	**Network Bytes Total**	This counter shows the bytes per second that are sent and received on the NIC
	Network Bytes Received/sec	This counter shows the bytes per second that are received on the NIC
	Network Bytes Sent/ sec	This counter shows the bytes per second that are sent from the NIC

Chart features	Counters	Description
Virtual Network Usage (Bytes)	Virtual Network Bytes Sent/sec	This counter shows the number of bytes per second that are sent over the network shown
	Virtual Network Bytes Received/sec	This counter shows the number of bytes per second that are received from the network
	Virtual Network Bytes/sec	This counter shows the number of bytes per second that are sent and received over the network
Virtual Network Usage (Packets)	Virtual Network Packets Sent/sec	This counter shows the number of packets sent per second on the network adapter
	Virtual Network Received/sec	This counter shows the number of packets received per second on the network card
Legacy Network Bytes Dropped	Legacy Network Bytes Dropped	This counter shows the number of bytes dropped by the network card
Legacy Network Usage	Legacy Network Bytes Sent/sec	This counter shows the bytes per second that are sent by the network card
	Legacy Network Bytes Received/sec	This counter shows the bytes per second that are received on the network card

The Virtual Switch performance chart

The **Virtual Switch** performance chart shows the switch performance statistics for the virtual switch used by the guest machines.

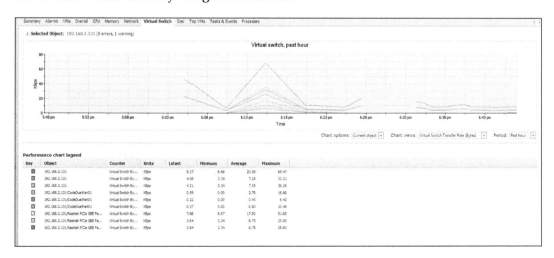

The Disk performance chart

The **Disk** performance chart shows all of the statistics for the hard drive partitions on each selected virtual machine object.

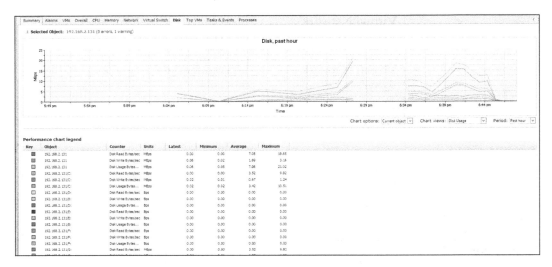

Viewing the dashboards when monitoring

The Veeam® ONE™ dashboards are used to review information at a glance that has been collected from the virtual machine host servers. It displays the current state of the virtual environment.

1. Let's begin by opening the Veeam® ONE™ Reporter application. Double-click on the **Veeam ONE Reporter** desktop icon.

2. Open the **Dashboards** tab. Note that the order of the displayed dashboards can be rearranged by dragging their images to a different position.

3. Open the dashboard widget by clicking on the dashboard image. Note that you can also open the dashboard widget by clicking on the **View** link located at the lower-left corner of the widget, or by opening the menu at the upper-right corner of the dashboard page and clicking on the **View** dashboard.

Adding dashboards

To create a dashboard, you will need to select the dashboard settings and widgets as follows:

1. Click on the **Dashboards** view tab, scroll down to the bottom of the console, and click on the plus button in the empty widget cell.

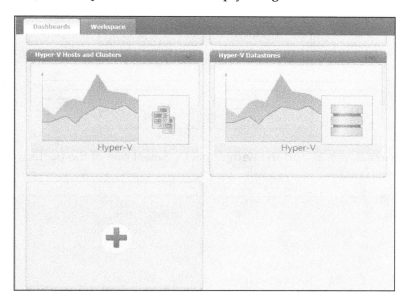

2. Enter the name and description for the new dashboard.

3. Choose how many layout items need to be displayed. Then click on **OK**.

4. Now that you have created the dashboard, the next step is to add the widget. Click on the plus button in one of the empty widget cell areas. This will open the **Add widget** wizard.

5. The first step is to add the widget packs. Select one of the packs in the list and click on **Next**.

6. Choose the widget that you want added to the dashboard. Then click on **Next**.

> Once you click on each widget, you will be given a preview of how the widget will look in the dashboard and a hint of what information is analyzed and displayed in the widget.

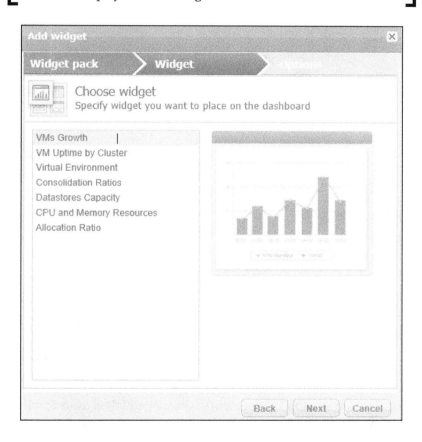

7. Under the **Options** tab, define the widget scope. Choose the scope for the widget data collection. You will have two options when setting the data for the widget.

At this stage, the first option is to process data from the Veeam® **Backup & Replication** infrastructure objects, which is used from the data protection widget.

The second option is to process data from the **Virtual Infrastructure** objects, which is used for the virtual environment widget.

8. Click on **Finish** to create the new dashboard widget.

Deleting dashboards

In **Veeam ONE Reporter**, it is very simple to delete a custom dashboard. However, when you remove a dashboard, it is not permanently deleted. The dashboard is first archived so that you are able to restore it at a later time. Perform the following steps to learn how to delete dashboards:

1. Open **Veeam ONE Reporter** and select the dashboard that you would like to remove from the **Dashboards** view.

2. Click on the right corner of the dashboard. Click on **Delete**.

Editing dashboards

With **Veeam ONE Reporter**, it is easy to edit the properties of a custom dashboard. To edit the board properties, perform the following steps:

1. Click on the **Veeam ONE Reporter** shortcut and click on the right corner of the dashboard.

2. Click on the **Edit dashboard** option in the menu items.

3. Make changes to the required dashboard properties (name and layout).

4. Click on **OK** to save the changes.

Configuring notifications

The Veeam® ONE™ Monitor tool is a great tool that can be used to ensure that you do not miss critical events or changes that happen in your environment. You can configure the Veeam® ONE™ Monitor tool to send e-mail notifications when a specific event is triggered, but the drawback is you can end up getting an excessive amount of e-mails if the notifications are not tuned properly. Perform the following steps to learn how to configure the notifications for Veeam® ONE™ alerts:

1. Double-click on the **Veeam ONE Monitor** desktop icon.

2. As you open up Veeam® ONE™ Monitor for the first time, **Configuration Wizard** will appear. These settings are used for sending the e-mail notifications and SNMP traps. However, if you decide to skip the **Configuration Wizard** during the initial setup, this wizard can be found in the options under the server settings.

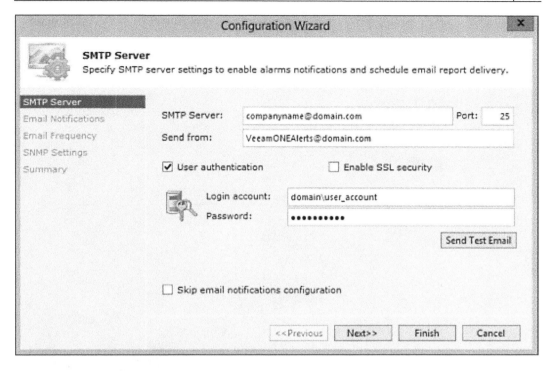

3. Enter the DNS name or IP address in the **SMTP Server** field. Change the port to match the SMTP communication port for your SMTP e-mail server if necessary.

4. Enter the e-mail address of the notification sender, for example, VeeamONEAlert@domain.com.

5. If your SMTP server requires authentication or SSL security, check the **User authentication** checkbox or the **Enable SSL security** checkbox if necessary. Then import the **Login account** and **Password** information.

 To check whether the settings have been configured properly, click on the **Send Test Email** button.

6. Click on **Next**. Then, enter any additional e-mail recipients and click on the **Add** button. Change the notification state as follows:

   ° **Errors and Warnings**: An e-mail will be sent only if the error and warning status changes

   ° **Errors Only**: An e-mail will be sent for only the error status changes

   ° **Any State**: An e-mail will be sent anytime the alarm status changes to **Error**, **Warning**, or **Info**

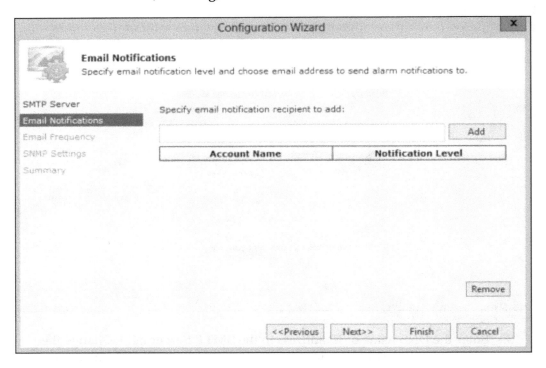

7. Click on **Next**. Highlight the **Mission Critical** notification policy. Then, click on the **Edit** button to make changes to the e-mail policy.

   The Veeam® ONE™ Monitor tool has two types of notification policies as follows:

   ° **Mission Critical**: This policy sends an e-mail notification immediately after a new alarm is triggered. This allows you to be notified instantly when a problem occurs.

   ° **Other**: This policy allows you to configure a specific delay or interval for the triggered alarms sent to your e-mail. This option can be used to prevent you from receiving e-mail notifications for false alarms. For example, if you planned to have 100 servers rebooted for maintenance purpose on a certain day, you would set an e-mail notification interval of 30 minutes before you were notified that a server was off the network or unavailable. This ensures that you will not receive unwanted e-mails for noncritical events.

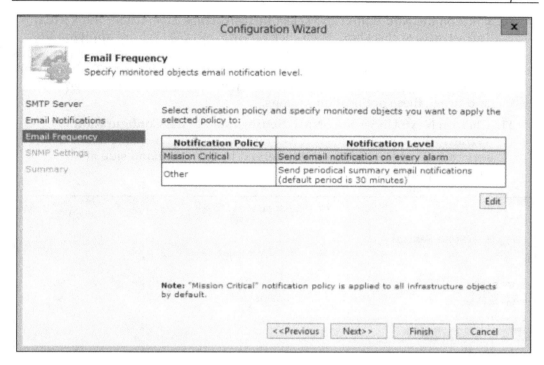

8. Remove the **Backup Infrastructure** and **vCloud Infrastructure** infrastructure objects since we will deal with only **Virtual Infrastructure** in this book. Then click on **OK**.

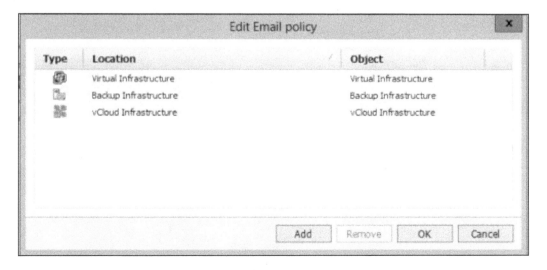

9. Highlight the **Other** notification policy and click on the **Edit** button.

10. Click on the **Add** button and select **Infrastructure Tree**. Check the **Virtual Infrastructure** checkbox. Then click on **Add** and **OK**. We are applying the e-mail frequency policy for **Other** to all the virtual infrastructure objects. This will prevent the initial overload of e-mails sent from Veeam® ONE™ as you deploy it to your virtual environment. After a few weeks, you can go back and tweak these notification settings.

11. Click on **Next**. Under the **SNMP Settings** step in the **Configuration Wizard** window, enter the receiver number which is the DNS name server or IP address of the SNMP server. In the right-hand side field, enter the port number.

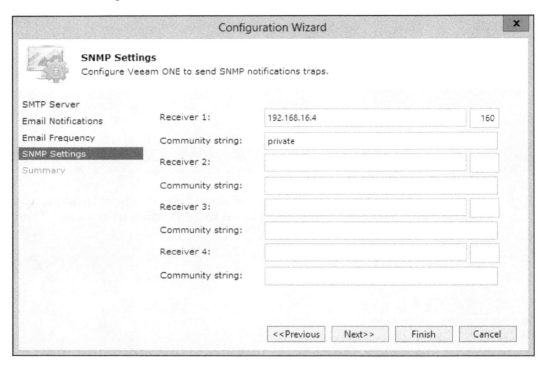

12. Click on **Next** to continue. Review the summary information and click on **Finish**.

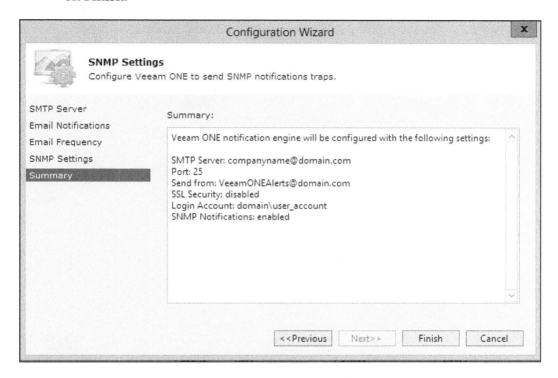

You have now finished configuring the notifications. It is not uncommon for systems administrators to turn off the e-mail notification feature shortly after they enable it due to the surge of e-mails that they receive. However, it is a great tool to have to monitor high availability systems while you are away from the office. This will allow multiple people to be contacted if a system goes down.

Summary

This chapter explained the process of configuring the Veeam® ONE™ Monitor tool. You were able to set up the monitoring tasks and events, view the dashboards, and configure the notifications. In the next chapter, we will discuss how to configure the Veeam® ONE™ reports. The reporting feature is a great add-on to the Veeam® ONE™ application. Being able to configure reports will allow you to obtain summarized information from your environment.

3

Configuring Veeam® ONE™ Reports

Veeam® ONE™ reporting allows system administrators to perform tasks such as discovering virtual machines that have underutilized or overutilized CPU, disk space, networks, and memory resources. Also, reporting provides vital reports to key business areas on the availability of high-availability systems. For example, if a virtual machine was left in a powered off state, the Veeam® ONE™ reporting feature can be used for auditing purposes to find out the specific period of time the virtual machine was offline. This chapter will explain the process of saving, viewing, and configuring Veeam® ONE™ reports. In this chapter, we will discuss the following topics:

- Accessing Veeam® ONE™ Reporter
- Using dashboards to view reports
- Handling reports—saving, viewing, and scheduling

Ways to access Veeam® ONE™ Reporter

To locally access Veeam® ONE™ Reporter, you need to go to the **Programs** menu of Windows.

Veeam® ONE™ Reporter can be accessed from the desktop or Windows **Programs** menu. Select the Veeam® ONE™ Reporter shortcut link from the desktop or the **Programs** menu.

To remotely access Veeam® ONE™ Reporter, all you need to do is access it via a web browser.

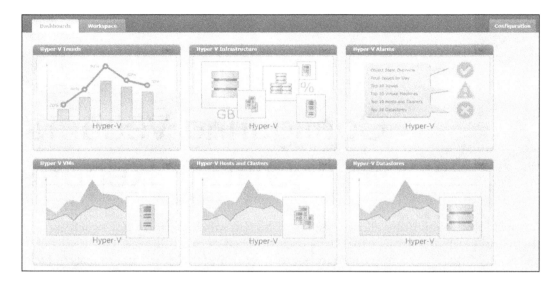

Open an Internet browser and type the following link (using the default TCP port 1239) to view the Veeam® ONE™ Reporter console:

```
http://<veeam one server name>:1239
```

[Make sure that the Veeam® ONE™ Reporter site is added to the list of trusted sites for Internet Explorer and pop-ups are allowed.]

Viewing the work areas for Veeam® ONE™ Reporter

Veeam® ONE™ Reporter has three working areas to review the reports: **Dashboards**, **Workspace**, and **Configuration**:

- **Dashboard**: This area includes modules called widgets, which are used to view the current health, performance, and configuration information
- **Workspace**: This area provides analysis information so that we can view the past performance, health statistics, and configuration for servers in the virtual environment

- **Configuration**: This area connects with the remote servers to perform administrative tasks

Changing the default configuration settings

To update the default configuration settings for Veeam® ONE™ Reporter, perform the following steps:

1. Check the scheduled data collection.
2. Check the Veeam® ONE™ Reporter license.
3. Check the Veeam® ONE™ Reporter settings.
4. Check the extension models.
5. Check the data administration settings.
6. View the Veeam® ONE™ Reporter configuration summary.

Access the Veeam® ONE™ Reporter settings using the **Configuration** tab.

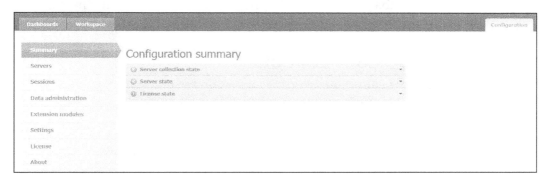

To view the **Summary** settings, click on the **Summary** link on the left-hand side pane. The **Configuration summary** page will reveal any configuration issue and show a brief overview of the settings in place. Some of the issues and warnings for the server state are as follows:

- The **Server collection state** option shows any warnings for the connected servers and results of the latest collection data.
- The **Server state** option shows the scheduling services.
- The **License state** option shows information about the status of the current license. It also has the option to install a new license.

Viewing the server configuration

To view the server configuration, click on the **Configuration** view and then click on the **Servers** link on the left-hand side pane, or click on **View details** from the **Server collection state** summary.

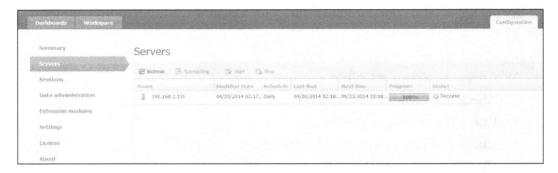

The data is automatically collected by setting up a schedule for specific virtual infrastructure servers. Change the collection mode to **Scheduled** and define the time settings by using the steps shown in the next section.

Scheduling the data collection

You can change the data collection schedule for certain host servers by performing the following steps:

1. Highlight the server.
2. Click on the **Schedule** button on the left-hand side of the window (previously greyed out).
3. Choose **Collect data automatically** or set a schedule, as appropriate.
4. Click on **OK** to accept the settings.

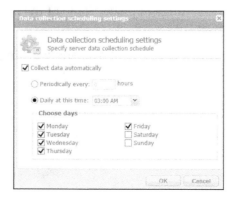

Performing a manual data collection

Veeam® ONE™ Reporter will start the collection session using the scheduled collection days and interval. However, if those collection periods are not set, you will need to perform the data collection manually. It is useful to do a manual collection if you have made an infrastructure change and you need real-time data.

Use the following steps to perform a manual data collection:

1. Open the **Servers** view on the left-hand side of the window.
2. Select the server for which you would like to run the data collection manually.
3. Then, click on the **Start** or **Stop** button on the toolbar.
4. Click on the **Sessions** tab to view the status of the manual collection and the past collection sessions.

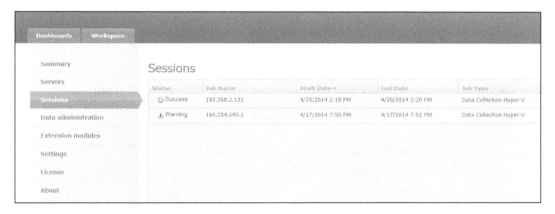

The data administration portion of the **Configuration** view gives you the ability to work with the archived dashboards and control the visibility of the connected virtual machines. When you delete a dashboard, Veeam® ONE™ Reporter places it in the dashboard archive instead of permanently removing it. Thus, using the restore feature of the dashboard archive, you are able to restore the previously deleted dashboards or completely remove them indefinitely.

To restore a previously deleted dashboard, perform the following steps:

1. Open the Veeam® ONE™ Reporter application.
2. Click on the **Configuration** link located in the upper-right corner.
3. Click on **Data administration**.
4. Open the **Dashboard archive** tab.

5. Click on the **Restore** link for the dashboard you wish to restore.

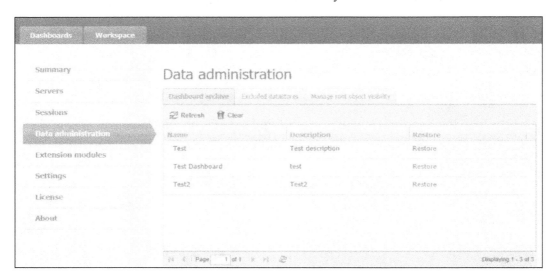

6. Click on **Yes** when prompted by a dialog box.

The dashboard is not actually deleted once you choose to remove it from the console. To permanently remove all the previously deleted dashboards, carry out the following steps:

1. Open the Veeam® ONE™ Reporter application.
2. Click on the **Configuration** link located in the upper-right corner.
3. Open the **Dashboard archive** tab.
4. Click on the **Clear** button.
5. Click on **Yes** when prompted by a dialog box.

Managing the root object visibility

As you remove a server object from Veeam® ONE™ Monitor, Veeam® ONE™ removes the server from the list of managed servers and removes the historical monitoring and categorization data for it as well. However, the historical reporting data is archived in the **Manage root object visibility** section. Thus, if you want to restore a removed server in the scope of a dashboard or report, it will have to be made available manually.

To show a previously removed server, perform the following steps:

1. Open the Veeam® ONE™ Reporter application.
2. Click on the **Configuration** link located in the upper-right corner.
3. Open the **Dashboard archive** tab and click on **Data administration**.
4. Click on the **Manage root object visibility** tab.
5. To make a server available, click on **Show**.

Now, the server will be displayed in the **Workspace** and **Dashboards** views.

Changing the extension modules

The extension modules are additional elements that can be optionally deployed to enhance the features of Veeam® ONE™ Reporter. The following three modules are available:

- **Hotfix pack**: This module shows the possible Veeam® ONE™ hotfixes
- **Widget pack**: This module shows a set of widgets
- **Report pack**: This module shows a set of reports

The **Extension modules** section of the **Configuration** view displays a list of extension modules. To install a new module, click on the **Install** button and specify a local path to the module.

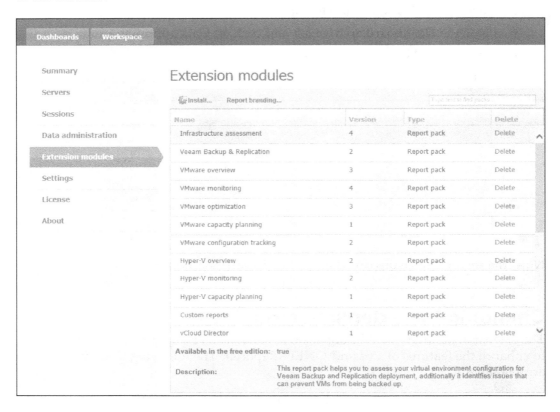

Viewing the general settings of Veeam® ONE™ Reporter

The general settings of Veeam® ONE™ can be adjusted as follows:

- Use the **SSRS Server** tab to change the SQL reporting services server
- Use the **SMTP Server** tab to change the settings for sending e-mails
- Use the **Email Notification** tab to change the general notification settings

Read the next section to get in-depth information about the points mentioned.

Adjusting the SSRS server settings

The **SSRS Server** settings are used to change the preferences for the Microsoft SQL reporting services server that is integrated with Veeam® ONE™ Reporter.

To adjust the SSRS server settings, perform the following steps:

1. Click on the **Use the Microsoft SQL Server Reporting Services** checkbox.

2. Enter the address of the SSRS server in the **SSRS server URL** field. Use the following format: `http://servername:port/VirtualDirectory`.

3. Enter the username and password used to connect to the SSRS server.

4. Click on the **Test Connection** button to verify the SSRS connection settings option.

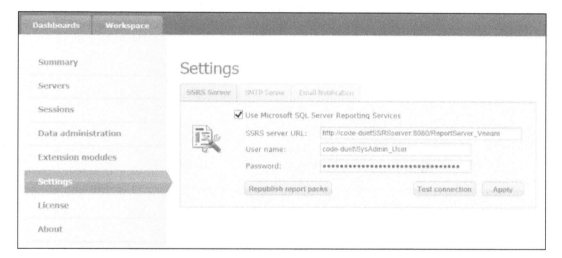

The SMTP server settings

The SMTP server settings are used to specify the e-mail settings, which are used to schedule the e-mailed reports and notifications.

 If the settings for the SMTP server were already configured using Veeam® ONE™ Monitor, you can skip this step. The changes will be propagated to Veeam® ONE™ Reporter automatically.

To manage the SMTP server settings, perform the following steps:

1. Enter the hostname or IP address of the SMTP server in the **SMTP server** field.

2. Enter a sender e-mail address in the **From** field.

3. Type the necessary credentials to authenticate the SMTP server.

4. Change the TCP port and select **Use SSL** to enable the SSL encryption if necessary.

5. Click on **Test Connection...** to verify the e-mail settings. Enter an e-mail address that can be used for receiving the test e-mail. Click on the **Send** button.

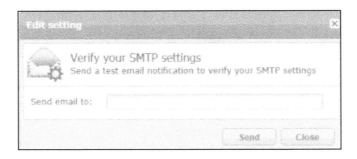

6. Click on **Apply** to save the settings.

The e-mail notification settings

In order to receive the e-mail notifications from the Veeam® ONE™ report data collection, you will need to enable the notification features. To enable the notification features, you need to perform the following steps:

1. Click on the **Configuration** link located in the upper-right corner.

2. Select the **Settings** link.

3. Click on the **Email Notification** tab.

4. Select the **Enable e-mail notifications for data collection sessions** checkbox.

5. Enter the recipient's e-mail address in the **To** field. Add multiple addresses, separating each address with a semicolon.

6. Enter the e-mail subject in the **Subject** field, referring to the following details:

    ° `%ServerName%`: This variable sets the name of the server from which the data was collected

    ° `%Result%`: This variable sets the status of the data collection or result of the job used for the scheduled report

    These variables work as placeholders for the server name and the information collected by Veeam® ONE™. They will be replaced with the actual data returned from the job.

7. Select the incidents that will trigger the e-mail notifications (**failure**, **warning**, or **success**). A log is attached to the e-mail message containing the detailed summary. Also, the body of the message will include the description and completion report for the event.

8. Send a test message by clicking on the **Send test message** button and specifying a recipient.

9. Click on **Apply** to save the settings.

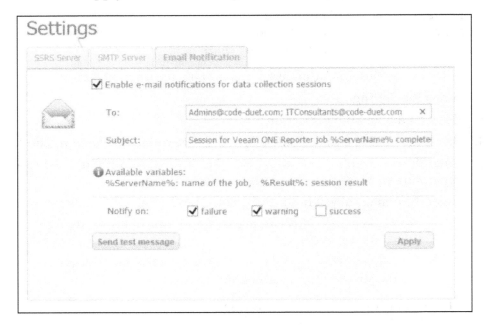

Using dashboards to view reports

The Veeam® ONE™ Reporter dashboard aggregates data used by system administrators to focus on the critical areas of the virtual environment. It comes with six predefined dashboards and core widgets used to deploy the reporting charts, tables, and graphs.

Viewing dashboards

To view the dashboards, you need to perform the following steps:

1. Click on the dashboard image.
2. Click on the **View** link located in the lower-left corner of the dashboard image.

Several widgets will be displayed, each in a separate cell in the dashboard. The reports are shown in an easy-to-comprehend report view.

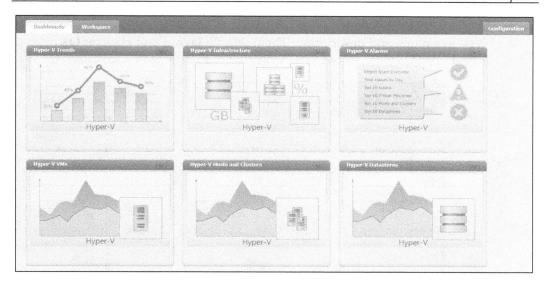

Creating dashboards

The following steps will explain the process of creating new dashboards:

1. Scroll to the bottom of the **Dashboards** window.

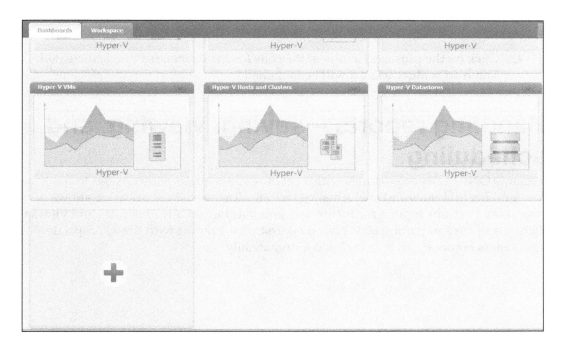

2. Click on the plus icon.

3. Type in a name and description. Then, select a layout and click on **OK**. A dashboard will be automatically created with an empty widget.

4. Click on the plus icon in one of the cells for the dashboard you just created. The **Add widget** wizard will be launched.

Handling reports – saving, viewing, and scheduling

Veeam® ONE™ Reporter comes with a set of ready-made reports created to track common health issues and performance factors. However, the workspace allows you to save various reports for future use, and it automatically generates and views them using custom parameters. You must first save a report with the appropriate parameters before it can be scheduled automatically.

Saving reports

To save a report, perform the following steps:

1. Open the **Workspace** tab.
2. Select the report you need to save from the **All folders** hierarchy.

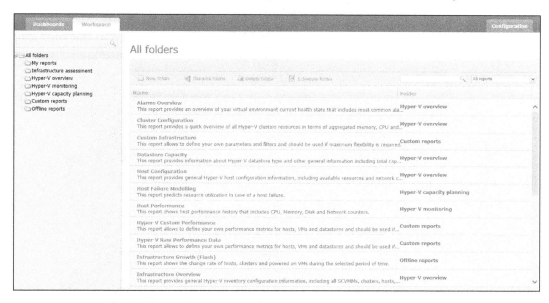

3. Select the parameters. Parameters are special variables used by Veeam®
    ONE™ Reporter to collect information specified by the person running
    a particular report.
4. Click on the **Save as...** button in the lower-right corner.

5. Type a name, folder location, and description for the report. Then, click on **OK**.

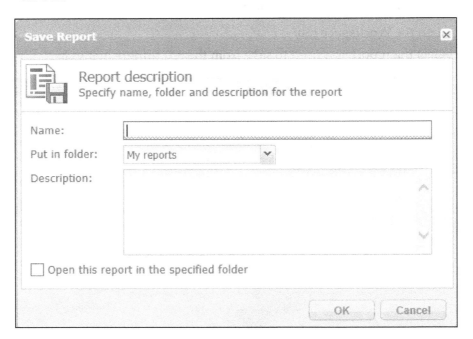

 Click on the **Open this report in the specified folder** checkbox if you need the report opened immediately after it is saved.

Viewing reports

To modify the previous reports that were saved, perform the following steps:

1. Open the **Workspace** view.
2. Select the necessary folder.
3. Select the report that you would like to make changes to.

4. Navigate to the **Actions** pane on the right-hand side and click on **Edit**.

5. Make changes to the report.
6. Navigate to the **Actions** pane and click on **Save**.

Scheduling reports

Reports can be automatically scheduled for delivery to a network share or hard drive. The created reports will have the most recent information about the virtual infrastructure.

To schedule reports, perform the following steps:

1. Open the **Workspace** tab view.
2. Select the report that you need scheduled under **My Reports**.
3. Click on the saved report. Then, navigate to the **Actions** pane and click on **Scheduling**.

4. In the **Scheduling** window, choose the report options (schedule, recipient, and the format).

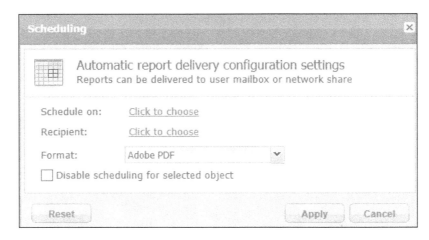

In the preceding screenshot, we can see the following fields:

° **Schedule on**: This field defines how often the report will be generated. You have the options to generate reports periodically (every hour), daily, or monthly. For example, you can have a report created automatically every Wednesday at 1:00 PM.

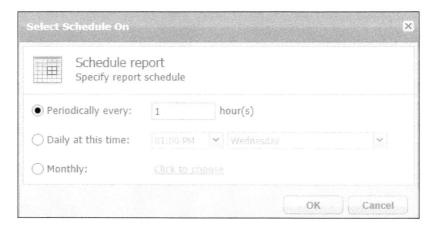

° **Recipient**: This field defines who will receive the report. You are given the option to select whether you would like the report to be sent to an e-mail address, hard disk, or network share.

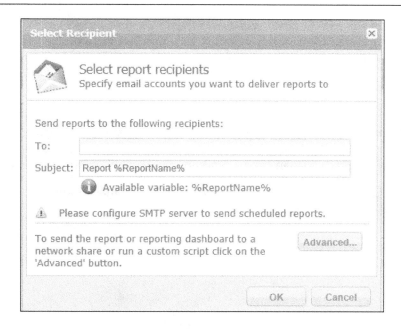

- ○ **Format**: This field defines how the report will be viewed. For example, you are given the option to have the report generated in the Adobe PDF, Microsoft Excel, or Microsoft Word file format.

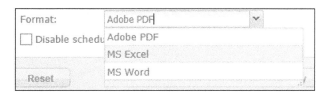

5. Click on **Apply** to accept the scheduling.

Scheduling automatic reports allows you to streamline the data collection from virtual machine objects in your infrastructure. It is also a great tool for auditing your virtual environment and creating a baseline for performance milestones. Custom reports are useful for data mining or analyzing different perspectives of the information returned and for creating relationships that can be useful for numerous projects, such as cost cutting or infrastructure capacity planning.

As explained in the next chapter, Veeam® ONE™ Business View can be leveraged to display categorized information about VMs and other virtual objects for planning, control, and analytics.

Summary

This chapter explained the process for saving, viewing, and configuring Veeam® ONE™ Reporter. We discussed the steps to access Veeam® ONE™ Reporter, used dashboards to view reports, and discussed how to save, view, and schedule reports.

In the next chapter, we will discuss Veeam® ONE™ Business View and the concepts to analyze the virtual environment.

4

Veeam® ONE™ Business View

Veeam® ONE™ Business View allows you to group and manage your virtual infrastructure in business containers. This is helpful to split machines into function, priority, or any other descriptive category you would like. Veeam® ONE™ Business View displays the categorized information about VMs, clusters, and hosts in business terms. This perspective allows you to plan, control, and analyze the changes in the virtual environment. The following topics will be discussed in this chapter:

- Data collection
- Model categorization
- Collecting data from VMs
- Exporting data to Excel

Data collection

The data required to create the business topology is periodically collected from the connected virtual infrastructure servers. The data collection is usually run at a scheduled interval. However, you can also run the data collection manually.

By default, after a virtual infrastructure server is connected to Veeam® ONE™, the collection is scheduled to run on a weekday at 2 a.m. If required, you can adjust the data collection schedule or switch to the manual collection mode to start each data collection session manually.

Scheduling the data collection

The best way to automate the collection of data is by creating a schedule for a specific VM server. To change the collection mode to **Scheduled** and to specify the time settings, use the following steps:

1. Open the Veeam® ONE™ Business View web application by either double-clicking on the desktop icon or connecting to the Veeam® ONE™ server using a browser with the URL `http://servername : 1340 by default`.

2. Click on the **Configuration** link located in the upper-right corner of the screen.

3. Click on the **VI Management Servers** menu option located on the left-hand side of the screen.

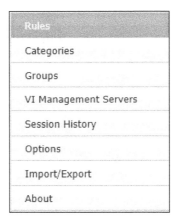

4. Select the **Run mode** option for the server that you would like to change the schedule for.

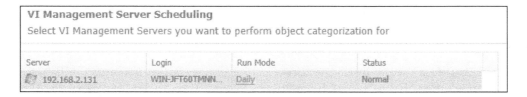

5. While scheduling the data collection for the VM server, perform the following steps:

　　° Select the **Periodically every** option if you plan to run the data collection at a desired interval

　　° Select the **Daily at this time** option if you plan to run the data collection at a specific time of the day or week

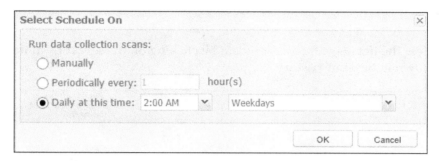

6. Once the schedule has been created, click on **OK**.

Collecting data manually

The following steps are needed to perform a manual collection of the virtual environment data. Use this procedure to collect data manually:

1. Click on the **Session History** menu item on the left-hand side of the screen.

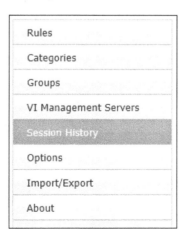

2. Click on the **Run Now** button for the server that you wish to run the data collection manually. The data collection normally takes a few minutes to run. However, it can vary based on the size and complexity of your infrastructure.

3. View the details of the session data by clicking on the server from the list shown in **Session History**.

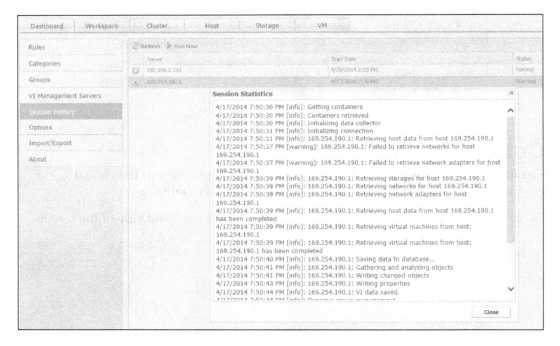

Model categorization

Veeam® ONE™ Business View comes out of the box with some predefined categories that you can use, such as **SLA**, **Storage Type**, **VMs with Snapshots**, and **Sample Business View Category**. The categories are useful to organize grouped Veeam® ONE™ infrastructure objects. After connecting the virtual servers and running the data collection, you will need to configure the categorization scheme by performing the following steps:

1. Create the categories.
2. Create the groups with each category used to specify the static or dynamic list of the VM objects that are being categorized.
3. Configure the categorization rules.
4. Synchronize the infrastructure mapping.

Creating categories

You are allowed to add up to 25 new categories in your virtual environment. Perform the following steps to add a new category:

1. Open the Veeam® ONE™ Business View application.
2. Click on the **Configuration** link in the upper-right corner of the screen.
3. Click on the **Categories** tab located on the left-hand side of the window.

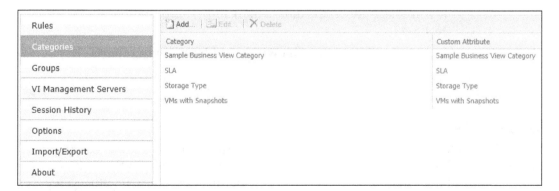

4. Click on the **Add...** button located above the category column.

5. Enter a friendly name, which will be the name of the category. Choose a custom attribute and set the group type to **Static** or **Dynamic**. Then, select an object type from the drop-down list (**Virtual Machine, Cluster, Host, Storage**, or **All**).

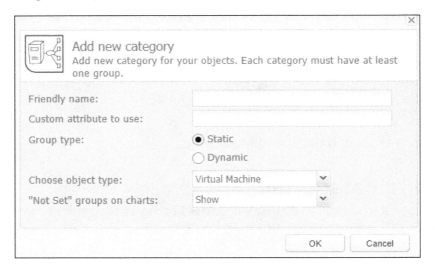

6. Next, you will need to choose whether to show or hide the data on the uncategorized objects:
   - If you select **Show**, the data will include charts and be labeled as **Not Set**
   - If you select **Hide**, the data will be hidden from the charts

7. Click on **OK** to add the new category.

Creating groups

You will need to configure the groups for each category after you finish creating the categories. There are two types of groups available in Veeam® ONE™ Business View — **Static** and **Dynamic**. However, you cannot mix these groups with a category:

- **Static**: This group is populated based on a manually assigned set of objects for a certain criteria

- **Dynamic**: This group is populated based on a predefined condition

The following steps will walk you through creating a static group:

1. Open the Veeam® ONE™ Business View application.
2. Click on the **Configuration** link in the upper-right corner of the screen.
3. Click on the **Groups** tab located on the left-hand side of the window.

4. Select the category under which you would like to add the group. All of the categories are shown as tabs.
5. Click on the **Add** button.
6. Enter a group name in the **Friendly Name** field. This will be the name displayed in the dashboard. Then, enter a custom attribute value and a description.

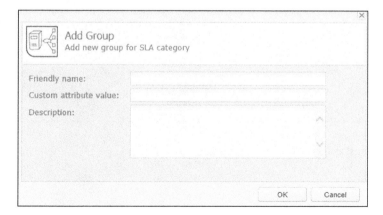

7. Click on **OK** to save the new group for the specified category.

The best way to automate the virtual infrastructure objects populated for static groups is by creating a categorization rule. A categorization rule is a condition used for a particular static group. Once the condition is met, the object is automatically added to the preset static group.

Configuring the categorization rules

The categorization rules are used instead of adding the virtual infrastructure objects to the static groups manually. A categorization rule is a condition that is run against the virtual server hierarchy. It allows you to filter and group objects by object name, infrastructure location, and object properties.

Instead of adding the virtual infrastructure objects to the static groups manually, you can create the categorization rules and assign them to the static groups.

A categorization rule is a condition with which objects in the virtual server hierarchy either comply or do not comply. The categorization rules can filter out and group objects by the following criteria: object name, infrastructure location, and object properties.

Perform the following steps to create a new categorization rule:

1. Open the Veeam® ONE™ Business View application.
2. Click on the **Configuration** link in the upper-right corner of the screen.
3. Click on the **Rules** tab.

4. Click on the **Create New...** button.

5. Enter a name and description for the rule being created, and then click on **Next**.

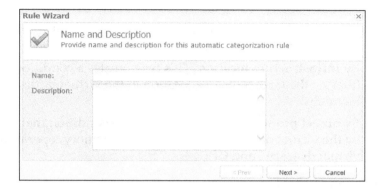

6. Select the type of virtual infrastructure object that this rule applies to (**Virtual Machines**, **Host Systems**, or **Storage**). Click on **Next** to continue.

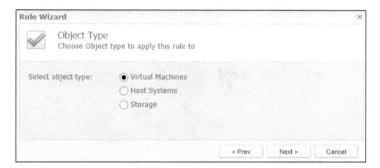

7. Click on the drop-down arrow to view the virtual environment hierarchy tree. Select the level of hierarchy on which the rule will be applied, and then click on **Next** to continue.

8. Select the type of rule being created (by object name, infrastructure location, or object properties). Click on **Next** to continue. Let's look at the categories:

   ○ **By object name**: This type creates a condition that will filter by the virtual infrastructure object names

   ○ **By infrastructure location**: This type creates a condition that will filter by the virtual object's location in the virtual infrastructure hierarchy

   ○ **By object properties**: This type creates a condition that will filter by the virtual object properties, such as memory, operating system, virtual disk size, and CPU

   The following should appear on your screen:

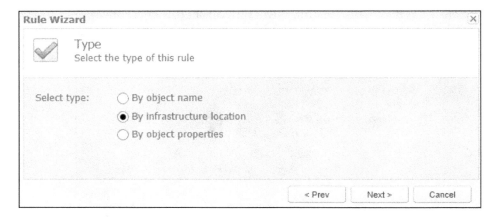

Now that you have specified the condition for the rule, if you select the **By object name** or **By object properties** option during the preceding step, you will need to configure the rule condition. However, if you choose the **By infrastructure location** type of rule, you will be skipped to the **Categorization** selection step. Click on **Next** continue.

If you chose to group objects by name, you will need to specify a text pattern for the object name.

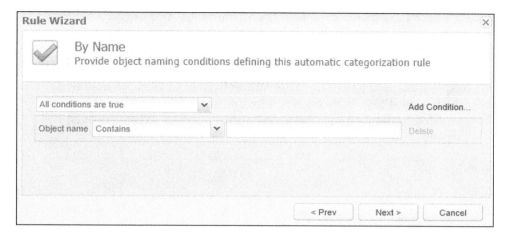

If you chose the **By Object properties** type, you will need to select an object property and choose a value that will be checked by the condition.

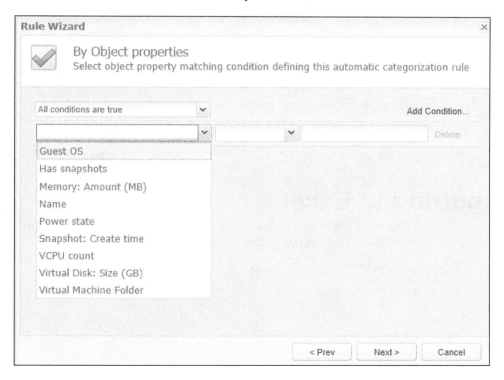

In the **Assign this group** drop-down list, select the category and group that includes the virtual infrastructure objects that match the specified conditions from the preceding step in **Rule Wizard**. Choose the **Apply Rule** option (**Automatically** or **Require manual approval**) on the basis of the following description:

- **Automatically**: This option is used to allow objects that match a condition to be added to a group as soon as they are discovered in the virtual hierarchy.

- **Require manual approval**: This option is used to allow objects that match a condition to be included in a group manually. The objects will be added to the **Require Approval** group in order to be approved by a system administrator.

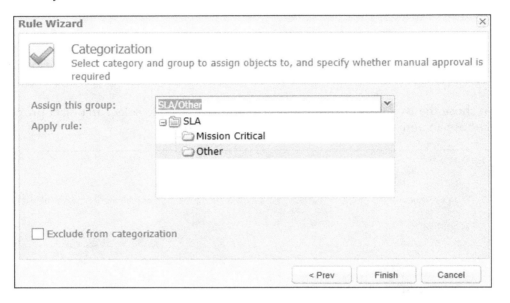

Exporting to Excel

Veeam® ONE™ Business View makes it easy to export the virtual infrastructure data to an XLS document. To export the data, perform the following steps:

1. Open the Veeam® ONE™ Business View application.

2. Open the **Workspace** tab.

3. Select a virtual infrastructure object. Click on the **Export to Excel** button in the upper-right corner of the screen.

4. Click on **Save** or open the Excel file.

The ability to export the virtual infrastructure object data is a great tool when you need to share or document the information in your virtual environment.

Summary

In this chapter, we explained Veeam® ONE™ Business View. We discussed the steps needed to plan, control, and analyze the changes in the virtual environment. In the next chapter, we will discuss the best practices of Veeam® ONE™ and common guidelines.

5
Best Practices

This chapter will explain the steps required to resolve the common issues in your virtual environment. It is essential to ensure that both the host and the guest systems have adequate disk space, RAM, and other resources needed to keep their performance stable. Veeam® ONE™ provides several monitoring methods that can be used to troubleshoot unnecessary services and alerts.

The following topics for best practices will be discussed in this chapter:

- Stopping unnecessary processes
- Setting up storage optimization
- Troubleshooting irregular CPU usage
- Turning off unnecessary alerts

Stopping unnecessary services

In the following task, we will go through the steps of stopping unnecessary processes that are utilizing too much of the CPU. These are the known processes that you have researched and noticed to run at a much lower CPU in the past. You can view the services running on a particular virtual machine by using the Veeam® ONE™ Monitor console. The steps are as follows:

1. Select **Virtual Machine** from the **Infrastructure** view.

2. Click on the **Processes** tab:

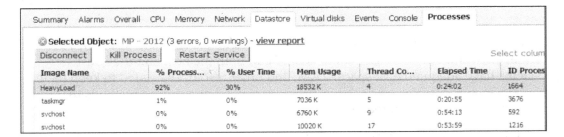

>
> Note that the **HeavyLoad** process uses 92 percent of the CPU, although it is known to consume 30 percent CPU on a consistent basis.

3. Select the process that needs to be stopped and click on the **Kill Process** button. Then, click on **Yes** to terminate the process.

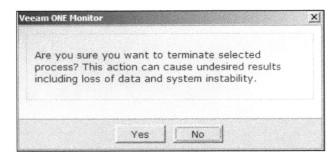

4. Click on the **Summary** tab to check the CPU monitor as shown in the following screenshot:

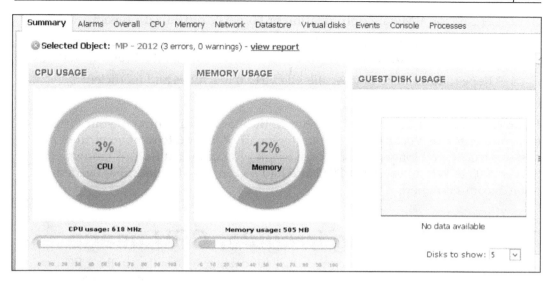

Setting up storage optimization

The following steps will discuss storage optimization and the procedure used to discover virtual machines that are idle, turned off, or overprovisioned resources. Storage optimization is the practice of adding storage to virtual machines that are low on disk space and lowering or removing storage on machines in your virtual environment that are rarely used. This is a preventative maintenance step used to properly reallocate storage resources and save the storage cost. You will run reports from the Veeam® ONE™ VMware optimization pack to find the idle virtual machines and over machines with inefficient storage use. The steps are as follows:

1. Open Veeam® ONE™ Reporter and navigate to the **Workspace** tab. The left pane of the **Workspace** tab contains a hierarchy of folders containing reports, as shown in the following screenshot. Then, click on the **Templates** menu item.

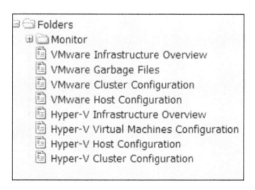

2. Locate the **VMware optimization** or **Hyper-V optimization** pack.

3. Next, we will locate the machines that were allocated too much disk space. Click on **Oversized Virtual Machines**. Then, click on the **Preview** button.

4. Repeat these steps to view the idle virtual machines and inefficient datastore usage.

In conclusion, you learned how to optimize the storage utilization in your virtual environment. This Veeam® ONE™ strategy will allow you to remove virtual systems that are no longer in use. For example, you migrated from Windows Server 2003 to Windows Server 2012 and had a group of machines that needed to be decommissioned.

Troubleshooting irregular CPU usage

The following steps will cover the procedure for dealing with spikes in the CPU usage. The common causes for the CPU spikes are misconfigured applications, excessive usage by too many users on one system, operating system issues, and processes left in a hung state by the legacy applications or backup applications. The steps are as follows:

1. Open the Veeam® ONE™ Monitor application and select the **Summary** tab.

2. Click on the virtual machine source with the VM CPU usage error:

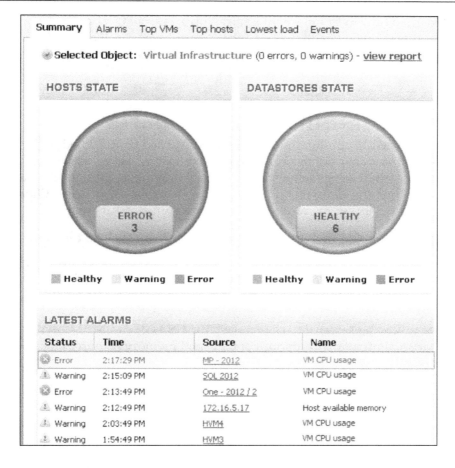

3. The **Alarms** tab will open. Click on the error and then check the alarm details:

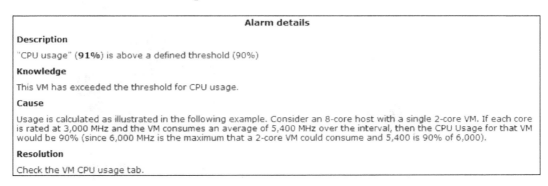

4. Open the **Processes** tab to view the CPU percentage for each process.

5. Choose the process with the issue and click on the **Kill Process** button.

You just learned how to troubleshoot issues with excessive CPU usage. In order to actively monitor system health, it is best that you subscribe to the e-mail alerts and set the threshold to a level that does not create false alerts. That way, you will be able to assess whether the systems with high CPU usage need immediate attention.

Turning off unnecessary alerts

Sometimes, you will encounter unnecessary alerts caused by the scheduled software updates, antivirus scans, and the applications that heavily use the system resources, such as Microsoft SQL or Symantec Backup. The following task will walk you through the steps of finding the alarm history and root cause for the alarm. In addition, the following steps will cover the procedure to suppress unnecessary alarms:

1. Open the Veeam® ONE™ Monitor console. Then, click on the **Summary** tab.

[Let's learn from an example issue with alerts caused by excessive CPU usage.]

The following screenshot shows the **CPU USAGE** and **MEMORY USAGE** charts that display the amount of CPU and memory resources the VM is currently consuming:

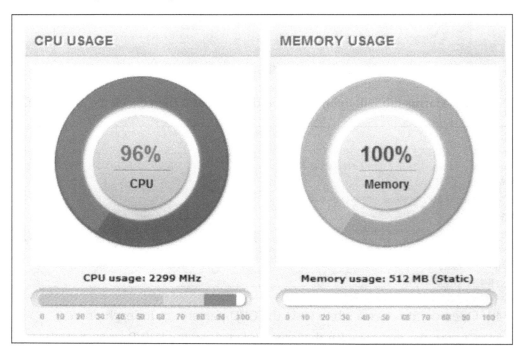

2. Click on the **Alarms** tab. Then select the error alert.

3. In the **Actions** pane, click on the **Show History** link. View and jot down the times at which the alert occurs.

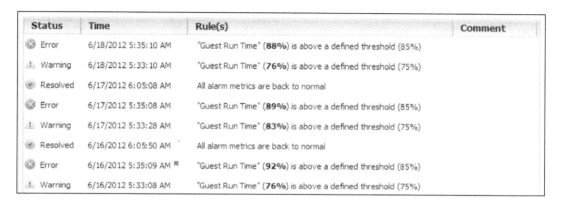

Status	Time	Rule(s)	Comment
⊗ Error	6/18/2012 5:35:10 AM	"Guest Run Time" (**88%**) is above a defined threshold (85%)	
⚠ Warning	6/18/2012 5:33:10 AM	"Guest Run Time" (**76%**) is above a defined threshold (75%)	
◉ Resolved	6/17/2012 6:05:08 AM	All alarm metrics are back to normal	
⊗ Error	6/17/2012 5:35:08 AM	"Guest Run Time" (**89%**) is above a defined threshold (85%)	
⚠ Warning	6/17/2012 5:33:28 AM	"Guest Run Time" (**83%**) is above a defined threshold (75%)	
◉ Resolved	6/16/2012 6:05:50 AM	All alarm metrics are back to normal	
⊗ Error	6/16/2012 5:35:09 AM	"Guest Run Time" (**92%**) is above a defined threshold (85%)	
⚠ Warning	6/16/2012 5:33:08 AM	"Guest Run Time" (**76%**) is above a defined threshold (75%)	

4. Click on the **Processes** tab and sort the data by the CPU percentage. Take a look at the process that is running with the highest CPU percentage.

5. Go back to the **Alarms** tab, click on the alarm, and click on **Edit** in the **Actions** pane.

6. In the **Alarms** window, navigate to the **Suppress** tab. Then, click on the **Suppress alarm during the following time period** radio button and select a time period to turn off the alarm. Click on **OK** to save the changes. It is recommended that you only suppress alarms for periods that are expected and regular.

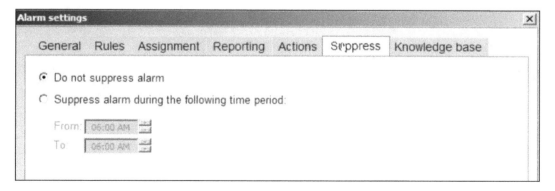

Alarm settings   ×

General   Rules   Assignment   Reporting   Actions   Suppress   Knowledge base

⦿ Do not suppress alarm

○ Suppress alarm during the following time period:

   From: 06:00 AM

   To   06:00 AM

Summary

In this chapter, you learned how to stop unnecessary services, set up storage optimization, troubleshoot irregular CPU usage, and turn off unnecessary alerts. The best practices that you learned will allow you to avert unforeseen issues in your environment.

Index

Thank you for buying
Managing Virtual Infrastructure
with Veeam® ONE™

About Packt Publishing

Packt, pronounced 'packed', published its first book, *Mastering phpMyAdmin for Effective MySQL Management*, in April 2004, and subsequently continued to specialize in publishing highly focused books on specific technologies and solutions.

Our books and publications share the experiences of your fellow IT professionals in adapting and customizing today's systems, applications, and frameworks. Our solution-based books give you the knowledge and power to customize the software and technologies you're using to get the job done. Packt books are more specific and less general than the IT books you have seen in the past. Our unique business model allows us to bring you more focused information, giving you more of what you need to know, and less of what you don't.

Packt is a modern yet unique publishing company that focuses on producing quality, cutting-edge books for communities of developers, administrators, and newbies alike. For more information, please visit our website at www.packtpub.com.

About Packt Enterprise

In 2010, Packt launched two new brands, Packt Enterprise and Packt Open Source, in order to continue its focus on specialization. This book is part of the Packt Enterprise brand, home to books published on enterprise software – software created by major vendors, including (but not limited to) IBM, Microsoft, and Oracle, often for use in other corporations. Its titles will offer information relevant to a range of users of this software, including administrators, developers, architects, and end users.

Writing for Packt

We welcome all inquiries from people who are interested in authoring. Book proposals should be sent to author@packtpub.com. If your book idea is still at an early stage and you would like to discuss it first before writing a formal book proposal, then please contact us; one of our commissioning editors will get in touch with you.

We're not just looking for published authors; if you have strong technical skills but no writing experience, our experienced editors can help you develop a writing career, or simply get some additional reward for your expertise.

Learning Veeam® Backup & Replication for VMware vSphere

ISBN: 978-1-78217-417-2   Paperback: 110 pages

Learn how to protect your data in your VMware vSphere infrastructure with Veeam® Backup & Replication

1. Explore Veeam® Backup and Replication v7 infrastructure and its components.

2. Create backup, replication, and restore strategies that protect data, your company's most valuable asset.

3. Includes advanced features like off-site replication and tape retention.

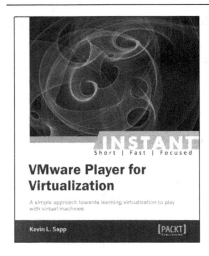

Instant VMware Player for Virtualization

ISBN: 978-1-84968-984-7   Paperback: 84 pages

A simple approach towards learning virtualization to play with virtual machines

1. Learn something new in an Instant! A short, fast, focused guide delivering immediate results.

2. Discover the latest features of VMware Player 5.0.

3. Evaluate new technology without paying for additional hardware costs.

4. Test your applications in an isolated environment.

Please check **www.PacktPub.com** for information on our titles

VMware Workstation – No Experience Necessary

ISBN: 978-1-84968-918-2   Paperback: 136 pages

Get started with VMware Workstation to create virtual machines and a virtual testing platform

1. Create virtual machines on Linux and Windows hosts.

2. Create advanced test labs that help in getting back to any virtual machine state in an easy way.

3. Share virtual machines with others, no matter which virtualization solution they're using.

VMware vSphere 5.x Datacenter Design Cookbook

ISBN: 978-1-78217-700-5   Paperback: 260 pages

Over 70 recipes to design a virtual datacenter for performance, availability, manageability, and recoverability with VMware vSphere 5.x

1. Innovative recipes, offering numerous practical solutions when designing virtualized datacenters.

2. Identify the design factors — requirements, assumptions, constraints, and risks — by conducting stakeholder interviews and performing technical assessments.

3. Increase and guarantee performance, availability, and workload efficiency with practical steps and design considerations.

Please check **www.PacktPub.com** for information on our titles